AFRICAN AMERICAN SU

PATRICK MAHOMES

PHIL CORSO

PowerKiDS press

New York

Published in 2022 by The Rosen Publishing Group, Inc.
29 East 21st Street, New York, NY 10010

Copyright © 2022 by The Rosen Publishing Group, Inc.

All rights reserved. No part of this book may be reproduced in any form without permission in writing from the publisher, except by a reviewer.

First Edition

Editor: Greg Roza
Designer: Rachel Rising

Photo Credits: Cover, p. 1 Adam Glanzman/Stringer/Getty Images Sport/Getty Images; pp. 4, 6, 8, 10, 12, 14, 16, 18, 20, 21 Woskresenskiy/shutterstock.com; pp. 4, 6, 8, 10, 12, 14, 16, 18, 20, 21 Sunward Art/shutterstock.com; p. 4 David Eulitt/Stringer/Getty Images Sport/Getty Images; p. 5 Justin Edmonds/Contributor/Getty Images Sport/Getty Images; pp. 7, 9 Christian Petersen/Staff/Getty Images Sport/Getty Images; pp. 11, 13 Icon Sports Wire/Contributor/Icon Sportswire/Getty Images; p. 15 Dustin Bradford/Contributor/Getty Images Sport/Getty Images; pp. 17, 19 Jamie Squire/Staff/Getty Images Sport/Getty Images; p. 20 Moses Robinson/Stringer/Getty Images Entertainment/Getty Images.

Library of Congress Cataloging-in-Publication Data

Names: Corso, Phil, author.
Title: Patrick Mahomes / Phil Corso.
Description: New York : PowerKids Press, 2022. | Series: African American superstars | Includes index.
Identifiers: LCCN 2020038364 | ISBN 9781725326194 (Library Binding) | ISBN 9781725326170 (Paperback) | ISBN 9781725326187 (6 pack)
Subjects: LCSH: Mahomes, Patrick, 1995–Juvenile literature. | Quarterbacks (Football)–United States–Biography–Juvenile literature. | African American football players–United States–Biography–Juvenile literature. | African American athletes–United States–Biography–Juvenile literature. | Kansas City Chiefs (Football team)–History–Juvenile literature. | Super Bowl–History–Juvenile literature.
Classification: LCC GV939.M284 C67 2022 | DDC 796.332092 [B]–dc23
LC record available at https://lccn.loc.gov/2020038364

Manufactured in the United States of America

CPSIA Compliance Information: Batch #CSPK22. For Further Information contact Rosen Publishing, New York, New York at 1-800-237-9932.

Find us on

CONTENTS

All in the Family. 4
Pat and the Pigskin. 6
New at School 8
Record Breaker. 10
Drafted! 12
Starting in the Pros 14
Another Broken Record 16
Super Bowl! 18
On and Off the Field 20
Glossary 22
For More Information 23
Index. 24

All in the Family

Patrick Mahomes was born in Tyler, Texas, in 1995. His father of the same name spent 11 seasons with Major **League** Baseball (MLB) as a pitcher. The younger Pat spent his early years playing football, baseball, and basketball.

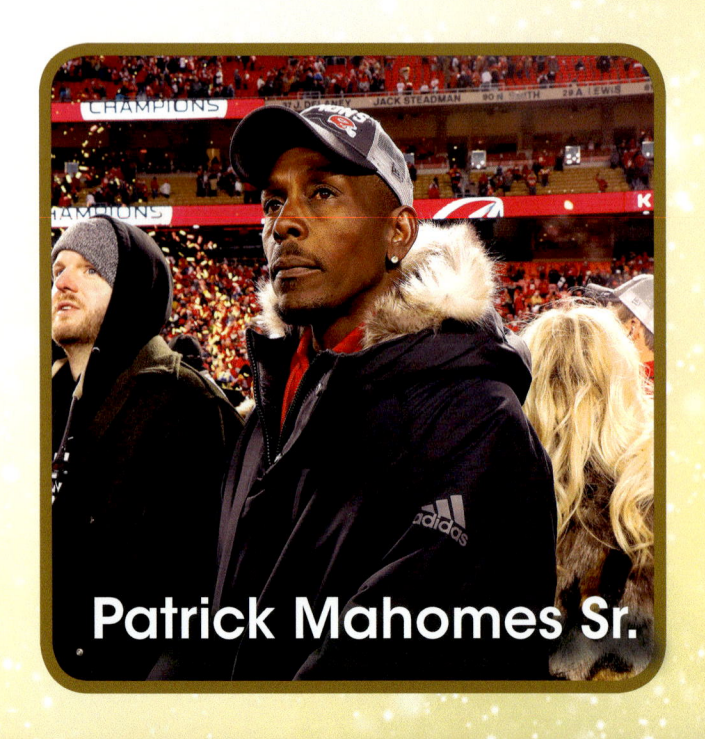

Patrick Mahomes Sr.

5

Pat and the Pigskin

Pat had early success in baseball. He was a star pitcher! However, he liked playing football more. As a quarterback in high school, Pat set records that will be hard to break. People around the country started hearing about the young **athlete**.

7

New at School

Mahomes attended Texas Tech University in 2014. At this time, Pat was selected by a **professional** baseball team to play for them! But he wanted to play football. He ended his freshman, or first, year as a college quarterback with 16 touchdowns!

9

Record Breaker

In his sophomore, or second, year with the Texas Tech Red Raiders, Pat became the starting quarterback. In his junior, or third, year, Pat started breaking college football records. Pat threw the ball for 734 yards in a single game!

11

Drafted!

In January 2017, Pat decided he wanted to play in the National Football League (NFL). He impressed football **scouts** and was expected to be **drafted** in the first round of the 2017 NFL draft. The Kansas City Chiefs selected him 10th in the draft!

OUR FUTURE IS NOW

#ChiefsDraft

PATRICK MAHOMES II
QB | TEXAS TECH

Starting in the Pros

On July 20, 2017, Pat signed a four-year contract with the Chiefs. The contract was worth $16.42 million! Pat didn't play in a game until December 2017. He helped lead his team to a 27–24 win in his first professional game.

15

Another Broken Record

Pat was named starting quarterback for the Kansas City Chiefs for the 2018 season. He quickly broke an NFL record for most touchdowns thrown during a quarterback's first three career games. He ended 2018 with the title of league **MVP**.

17

Super Bowl!

In 2020, Pat led the Chiefs to their first **championship** in 50 years! The Chiefs beat the San Francisco 49ers to win Super Bowl 54. The Chiefs had been losing, but Pat led them back by scoring 21 points. Pat was named MVP of the game! Pat led the Chiefs to another Super Bowl appearance in 2021.

19

On and Off the Field

In 2019, Pat started the 15 and the Mahomies **Foundation**. This group helps improve the lives of children. This includes healthcare, schooling, sports, and more. Patrick Mahomes has shown that he's an MVP on and off the field!

TIMELINE

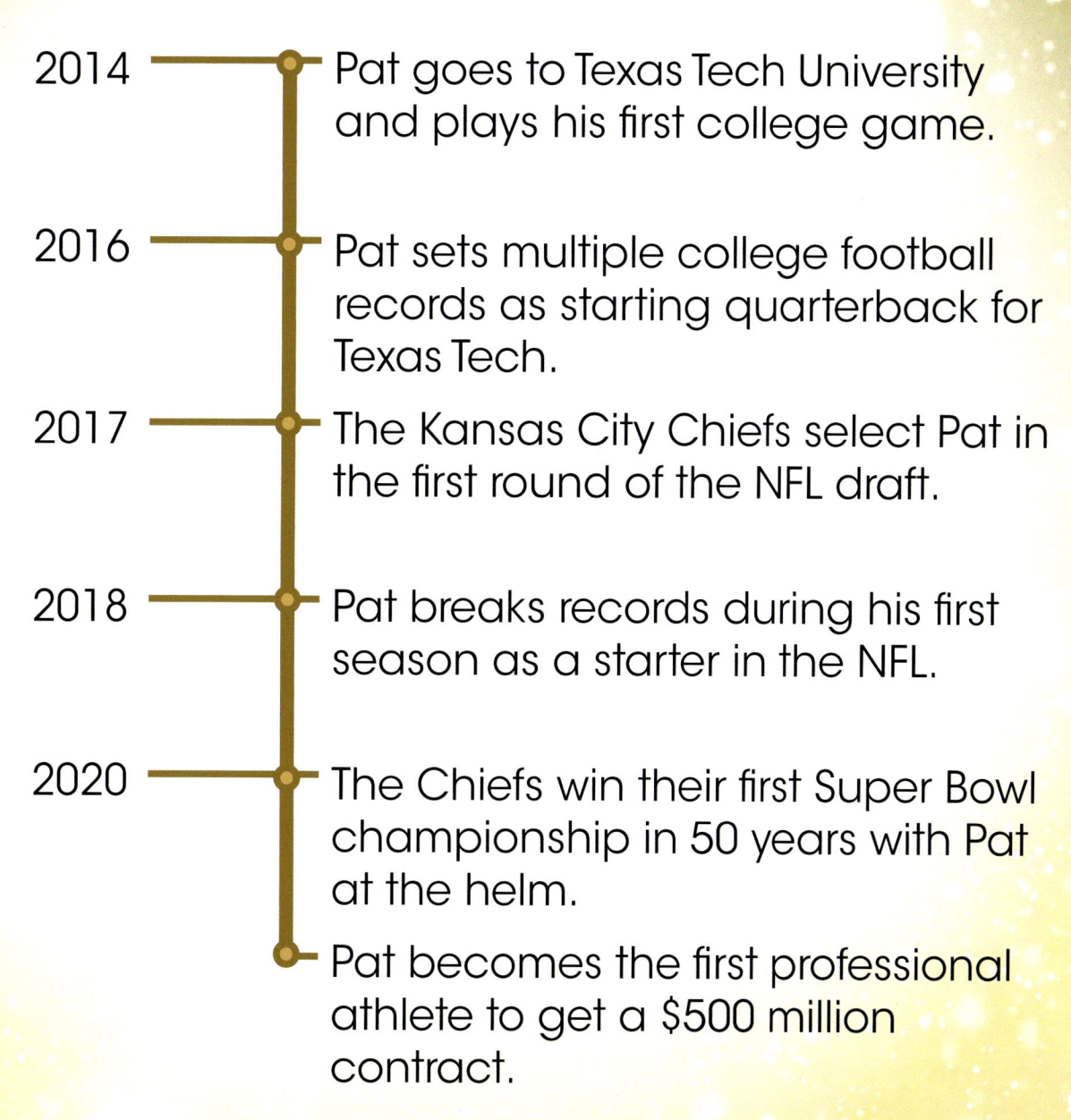

2014 — Pat goes to Texas Tech University and plays his first college game.

2016 — Pat sets multiple college football records as starting quarterback for Texas Tech.

2017 — The Kansas City Chiefs select Pat in the first round of the NFL draft.

2018 — Pat breaks records during his first season as a starter in the NFL.

2020 — The Chiefs win their first Super Bowl championship in 50 years with Pat at the helm.

— Pat becomes the first professional athlete to get a $500 million contract.

GLOSSARY

athlete: Someone who is good at sports and games that require physical skill and strength.

championship: A contest that decides which player or team is the best in a particular sport or game.

draft: To select a player for a team. Also the process of selecting players for a team or the related event.

foundation: A group created to support people in need with money or other benefits.

league: A group of sports teams that play each other one or more times during a season.

MVP: Most valuable player.

professional: Having to do with something done for money and not just for fun.

scout: Someone whose job is to watch young athletes in the hope of finding a new member for a team.

FOR MORE INFORMATION

BOOKS

Chandler, Matt. *Patrick Mahomes: Football MVP.* North Mankato, MN: Capstone Press, 2020.

Meggs, Chris. *Go Chiefs Go! The Championship Season of the Kansas City Chiefs.* Overland Park, KS: Ascend Books, 2020.

WEBSITES

15 and the Mahomies
www.15andthemahomies.org
Learn all about Mahomes's charitable foundation here.

National Football League
www.nfl.com
The NFL website features up-to-date information about the teams in the league and the league itself.

Publisher's note to parents and teachers: Our editors have reviewed the websites listed here to make sure they're suitable for students. However, websites may change frequently. Please note that students should always be supervised when they access the internet.

INDEX

A
baseball, 4, 6, 8
basketball, 4

D
draft, 12, 21

F
father, 4
15 and the Mahomies Foundation, 20

K
Kansas City Chiefs, 12, 14, 16, 18, 21

M
MVP, 16, 18, 20

N
National Football League (NFL), 12, 16, 21

Q
quarterback, 6, 8, 10, 16, 21

S
Super Bowl, 18

T
Texas Tech University, 8, 10, 21